Issue #2
Fall 2007

biography
for
beginners

Sketches for Early Readers

Laurie Lanzen Harris,
Editor

Favorable Impressions

P.O. Box 69018
Pleasant Ridge, Michigan 48069

Laurie Lanzen Harris, *Editor and Publisher*
Dan Harris, *Vice President, Marketing*
Laurie Collier Hillstrom, *Sketch Writer*
Catherine Harris, *Copy Editor*

Favorable Impressions
P.O. Box 69018, Pleasant Ridge, Michigan 48069

Printed in the United States

Contents

Preface

Biography for Beginners is a publication designed for young readers ages 6 to 9. It covers the kinds of people young people want to know about — favorite authors, television and sports stars, and world figures.

Biography for Beginners is published two times a year. A one-year subscription includes two 100-page hardbound volumes, published in Spring (May) and Fall (October).

The Plan of the Work

Biography for Beginners is especially created for young readers in a format they can read, understand, and enjoy. Each hardcover issue contains approximately 10 profiles, arranged alphabetically. Each entry provides several illustrations, including photographs of the individual, book covers, illustrations from books, and action shots. Each entry is coded with a symbol that indicates the profession of the person profiled. Boldfaced headings lead readers to information on birth, growing up, school, choosing a career, work life, and home and family. Each entry concludes with an address so that students can write for further information. Web sites are included as available. The length and vocabulary used in each entry, as well as the type size, page size, illustrations, and layout, have been developed with early readers in mind.

Because an early reader's first introduction to biography often comes as part of a unit on a writer like Dr. Seuss, authors are a special focus of *Biography for Beginners*. The authors included in this issue were chosen for their appeal to readers in grades one through four.

There is a broad range of reading abilities in children ages 6 to 9. A book that would appeal to a beginning first-grade reader might not satisfy the needs of an advanced reader finishing the fourth grade. To accommodate the widest range of readers in the age group, *Biography for Beginners* is written at the mid-second grade to third grade reading level. If beginning readers find the content too difficult, the entry could be used as a "read aloud" text, or readers could use the boldfaced headings to focus on parts of a sketch.

Indexes

Each issue of *Biography for Beginners* includes a Name Index, a Subject Index covering occupations and ethnic and minority backgrounds, and a Birthday Index. These indexes cumulate with each issue. The indexes are intended to be used by the young readers themselves, with help from teachers and librarians, and are not as detailed or lengthy as the indexes in works for older children.

Our Advisors

Biography for Beginners was reviewed by an Advisory Board made up of school librarians, public librarians, and reading specialists. Their thoughtful comments and suggestions have been invaluable in developing this publication. Any errors, however, are mine alone. I would like to list the members of the Advisory Board and to thank them again for their efforts.

Linda Carpino   Detroit Public Library
Detroit, MI

Nina Levine   Blue Mountain Middle School
Cortlandt Manor, NY

Nancy Margolin   McDougle Elementary School
Chapel Hill, NC

Deb Rothaug   Plainview Old Bethpage Schools
Plainview, NY

Laurie Scott   Farmington Hills Community Library
Farmington Hills, MI

Joyce Siler   Westridge Elementary School
Kansas City, MO

Your Comments Are Welcome

Our goal is to provide accurate, accessible biographical information to early readers. Let us know how you think we're doing. Please write or call me with your comments.

We want to include the people your young readers want to know about. Send me your suggestions to the address below, or to my e-mail address. You can also post suggestions at our website, www.favimp.com. If we include someone you or a young reader suggest, we will send you a free issue, with our compliments, and we'll list your name in the issue in which your suggested profile appears.

And take a look at the next page, where we've listed those libraries and individuals who will be receiving a free copy of this issue for their suggestions.

Acknowledgments

I'd like to thank Marco Di Vita for superb design, layout, and typesetting; Catherine Harris for editorial assistance; Barry Puckett for research assistance; and Kevin Hayes for production help. This issue is dedicated to the memory of Mary Ann Stavros-Lanning, who designed and typeset every issue of *Biography for Beginners*, from 1995 to Spring 2007.

Laurie Harris
Editor, *Biography for Beginners*
P.O. Box 69018
Pleasant Ridge, MI 48069
e-mail: laurieh@favimp.com
URL: http://www.favimp.com

In Memoriam

Mary Ann Stavros-Lanning

(1957-2007)

Artist, Designer, and Friend

Tim Berners-Lee
1955-
British Computer Scientist and Inventor
Inventor of the World Wide Web

TIM BERNERS-LEE WAS BORN on June 8, 1955, in London, England. His parents are Conway and Mary Berners-Lee. They are both computer scientists. They met while working on the first commercial computer. Tim has one brother, Peter.

TIM BERNERS-LEE GREW UP in London in a family that encouraged his talent for math. He and his brother used to play math games with imaginary numbers.

Tim loved computers. He built a cardboard model of the one his parents had created. He also loved trains, and had a model set. Fascinated by the way the trains worked, he created some electronic gadgets to run his set.

Tim also loved to read science fiction books. One particular favorite was a story called "Dial F for Frankenstein." It featured computers linked together that come "alive," acting and thinking on their own.

Tim also remembers a conversation he had with his dad when he was young. His dad said that computers would be so much more useful if, like the human brain, they could connect random pieces of information.

TIM BERNERS-LEE WENT TO SCHOOL at a private boys' school called Emmanuel. He was an excellent student. He went on to Queen's College, which is part of Oxford University. In college, he studied physics. "I thought science might turn out to be more practical than math," he says. He calls physics "halfway between math and electronics." And, for him, physics "turned out to be very special all of itself, and fascinating."

While in college, he couldn't use the university's computers. He'd broken the rules for student use of computers. So he bought an old TV set and made a computer out of it. "I soldered by hand every wire in it," he recalls. The machine was all his own. "Knowing it would do anything I had the imagination to program was a great feeling."

FIRST JOBS: After graduating from college in 1976, Berners-Lee got a job with a telecommunications company. He developed software. Software programs tell computers what to do. After two years, he moved on to another company, where he created typesetting software.

In 1980, Berners-Lee spent six months working as a software specialist for CERN. CERN is the world's major research institute for particle physics. Scientists from all over the world come to CERN, in Geneva, Switzerland, to work. While Berners-Lee was there, he developed a program, called "Enquire." It was an early attempt to link pieces of information.

INVENTING THE WORLD WIDE WEB: Berners-Lee began to work for CERN full time in 1984. He set out to solve a huge problem that kept the CERN scientists from being able to share information. "There was different information on different computers," he recalled. "But

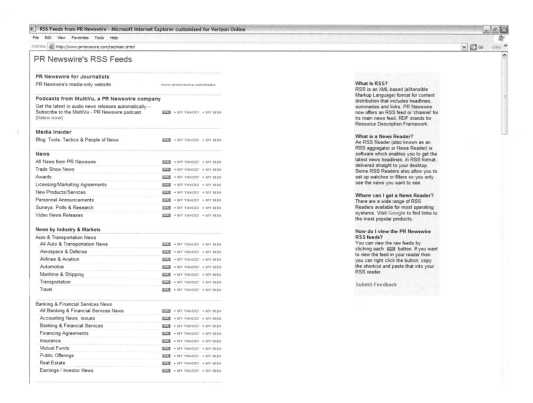

A page from the World Wide Web, created using HTTP protocol and HTML language, both created by Berners-Lee.

you had to log on to different computers to get at it." There was no universal computer language that the computers could share. So, there was no way for them to share information.

"I actually wrote some programs to take information from one system and convert it," he recalls. That got him to thinking of a universal solution to the problem. He asked himself, "Can't we convert every information system so that it looks like part of some imaginary information system which everyone can read? And that became the WWW," he explains.

THE INTERNET: The Internet and the World Wide Web are not the same thing. The Internet is a "network of networks." It was created in the 1970s by the U.S. military as a way to link computers around the world. It became popular in universities, too, as a means of transferring information. It was a global network, but the data it contained couldn't be searched and used easily.

Berners-Lee defined the challenge. He wanted to find a way to assign a *code* to documents. He needed to develop a system of rules that would *link* the documents. He needed to create a way to *identify* each document, in a universal language. His goal was to create a "single, global information space." In that space, "anything could be linked to anything." That "space" became the World Wide Web.

HTML, HTTP and URL: In 1990, Berners-Lee developed the *coding* system. He called it HyperText Markup Language (HTML). It is used to code text, pictures, and sound. This is the "language" people use to create hypertext Web pages. It is the language that's used for the hypertext "links" you click on to transfer between Web pages.

Next, Berners-Lee created HTTP. HTTP stands for HyperText Transfer Protocol. It's the communication standard that allows pages to be linked across the web. It also provides a standardized format, so the information on Web pages can be displayed and read.

Berners-Lee next created URLs. URL stands for Universal Resource Locator. It is the unique Web "address" for every Web page.

Berners-Lee named his project the "World Wide Web." He called it that to describe his vision of a web of information spanning the globe. It's the "www" you see in front of every Web address.

In 1991, Berners-Lee shared the program with the scientists at CERN. In the summer of 1991, he posted the software on the Internet. It became available to anyone who wanted it, for free.

Berners-Lee had created a browser, to allow searching, but it didn't utilize the "point and click" function (using a computer mouse) to activate hyperlinks. Marc Andreessen, founder of Netscape, developed a browser that could do that. Andreessen sold the software for the browser, becoming a millionaire in the process. The Web became easy to navigate, even for beginners. Millions of people began to use their computers to connect to the

Web. It was an explosion in information sharing, even greater than Berners-Lee had imagined. Today there are billions of Web pages, and millions of users, worldwide.

It's important to note that Berners-Lee never made money, or tried to patent, any of the technology that went into creating the World Wide Web. Instead, he thought it should be free to be shared by people everywhere. He knew that making money off his invention would create competitive products that would use different and incompatible systems. That would be the opposite of the universal source of communication he envisioned.

Berners-Lee has never wanted to be rich, or famous. "What is maddening is the terrible notion that a person's value depends on how important and financially successful they are," he says.

WORLD WIDE WEB CONSORTIUM: Today, Berners-Lee is head of the World Wide Web Consortium, or W3C. That is the group that coordinates the development of the Web. He works out of an office at the Massachusetts Institute of Technology (MIT), in Cambridge, Massachusetts.

Now, Berners-Lee is at work on a "semantic Web." That will allow documents on the Web to make sense to machines, not just people. He's creating a system to label information on Web pages that says what it is. This would allow information to be searched in a broader way. Right now, it's being used by science researchers to organize information from different fields.

TIM BERNERS-LEE'S HOME AND FAMILY: Berners-Lee is married to Nancy Carlson. They met while they were both working for CERN. They have two sons and live in the Boston area. He likes to keep his private life private, and asks people to respect that.

The World Wide Web has been a truly revolutionary force in modern life. It has changed the way people relate to one another and their world. Information, and

QUOTE

"Any really powerful thing can be used for good or evil. So what is made of the Web is up to us. You, me, everyone else. Here is my hope. The Web is a tool for communicating. The Web can help people understand each other. Let's use the Web to create neat, new, exciting things. Let's use the Web to help people understand each other."

the transmission of information, has always been a transforming force in society. The World Wide Web has allowed the free distribution of information in a way never before possible. And, as Berners-Lee says, it is still changing.

Berners-Lee hopes that the Web will be used for positive things.

FOR MORE INFORMATION ABOUT TIM-BERNERS-LEE:

Write: MIT Computer Science and Artificial Intelligence
Laboratory
The Stata Center, Bldg. 32
32 Vassar St.
Cambridge, MA 02139

WORLD WIDE WEB SITES:

http://www.time.com/time/time100/scientist/profile/
bernerslee.html

http://www.W3org/People/Berners-Lee/Kids

Miley Cyrus
1992-
American Actress and Singer
Star of "Hannah Montana"

MILEY CYRUS WAS BORN on November 23, 1992, in Nashville, Tennessee. Her parents are Billy Ray and Tish Cyrus. Billy Ray is a singer and actor and Letitia is a homemaker. Miley has five siblings. She has two half-brothers, Christopher and Trace, and a half-sister, Brandi. She has two younger siblings, too, named Braison and Noah.

Miley with her dad, Billy Ray Cyrus

"Miley" is a nickname. Her real name is Destiny Hope. Her dad gave her the nickname when she was a baby. He called her "Smiley" because she smiled all the time. Later, they dropped the "S" and just called her "Miley."

MILEY CYRUS GREW UP in a house full of family and music. She spent her first years on her family's 500-acre ranch near Nashville.

GETTING STARTED IN SHOW BUSINESS: Miley began to audition for shows when she was about 10. Her first TV role was in an episode of "Men in Tights." In 2006, she appeared in episodes of the hit TV show "The Suite Life of Zack and Cody." That same year, she got the role she's famous for, Hannah Montana, on the Disney Channel.

"HANNAH MONTANA": Miley's road to "Hannah Montana" wasn't easy. She first auditioned for the role when she was 12. The Disney executives thought she was too young. They continued to audition girls from all over. Miley really wanted the role. She decided to audition again. And this time, the Disney people knew she was the one.

In the show, Miley plays two roles: Miley Stewart, a regular teen growing up in Malibu, and Hannah Montana, a pop star. Her dual life is a secret, but the audience is in on the mystery. The show stars her real-life Dad, country star Billy Ray Cyrus, as her TV Dad. Her co-stars include Emily Osment and Jason Earles.

"Hannah Montana" is one of the top kids' shows in history. Miley's fans range in age from five to 12.

Miley as Hannah Montana

The cast of "Hannah Montana"

They come to her appearances in droves. Some even invite her to their birthday parties.

She's been mobbed by fans, which is a little scary, but funny, too. "It was weird the first time it happened," Miley recalls. "It was the day after the show came out. My best friend and I went to Universal and we heard these girls scream, 'Is it her?' We're looking around for Britney or Lindsay or someone famous. They're like, 'Are you Miley?' And I said, 'Miley? Yeah, why?' I thought I was in trouble."

HIT RECORDS: Miley is a genuine singing star, too. Her first album, "Hannah Montana," rose to Number 1 on the charts. Her second, "Hannah Montana 2/Meet Miley Cyrus" came out in June 2007 and made it to Number 1 in one week.

She's toured the country as part of the Cheetah Girls tour, and for her new records, too. She loves writing and performing. "I write all the time," she says. "Miley Cyrus wrote every song on that CD. I write in my sleep. I don't know how, but I'll work on a song, go to sleep, and it's finished when I wake up."

MILEY CYRUS GOES TO SCHOOL at a public school in California. She's tutored three hours a day on the set. She says she likes most of her subjects.

FUTURE PLANS: Miley hopes to stay in show business a long time. Recently, Disney launched a line of Hannah Montana clothing. And she'll be doing a feature film based on "Hannah Montana."

Still, her biggest love is music. "My music keeps me focused. I like the acting and the music, but the music is what's most important. I want to do that all my life."

MILEY CYRUS'S HOME AND FAMILY: Miley lives with her family in California. With her dad on the show, she sees a lot of him, and they are very close. "I feel I can tell my Dad anything," she says. "When we come home, we forget that we even work together and just hang out."

Miley's parents want her to have as normal a life as possible. So far, it looks like they're doing a good job. "The kid's been able to keep her head on her shoulders," says her Dad.

In addition to six kids, the Cyrus family includes six dogs, seven horses, and three cats. In her spare time, Miley likes to hang out with friends and shop.

FOR MORE INFORMATION ABOUT MILEY CYRUS:

Write: The Disney Channel
　　　　3800 West Almeda Ave.
　　　　Burbank, CA 91505

QUOTE

"I relate to the Miley character because that's kind of how I am when I'm not working. We go get ice cream down the street. I like my Miley life. When I go to the set I definitely feel like I'm living the script."

WORLD WIDE WEB SITES:

http://tv.disney.go.com/disneychannel/hannahmontana/
http://www.mileycyrus.com
http://www.mileyworld.com

Leo Dillon
1933-

Diane Dillon
1933-
American Authors and Illustrators
of Children's Books
Illustrators of *Why Mosquitoes Buzz*
in People's Ears and *Ashanti to Zulu*

LEO DILLON WAS BORN on March 2, 1933, in Brooklyn, New York. His full name is Lionel John Dillon. "Leo" is his nickname. His parents were Lionel and Marie Dillon.

They came to the United States from Trinidad before Leo was born. Lionel owned a trucking business and Marie was a dressmaker.

LEO DILLON GREW UP in Brooklyn, loving to draw. His parents encouraged his gift in every way. They had a good friend named Ralph Volman. He introduced Leo to the world of art. He was, Leo recalls, "a painter, a draftsman, a writer, a world traveler." Ralph took Leo to art shows, and got him supplies. He also critiqued and encouraged Leo in all his art work.

Leo loved to study illustrations in books. "I still have the one that changed my life," he recalls. *"The Arabian Nights*—I'd never before seen drawings of that quality." He visited his local library, captivated by the artwork he found in all kinds of books.

LEO DILLON WENT TO SCHOOL at the local public schools in New York. He went to the High School of Industrial Design. He remembers that one of his teachers, Benjamin Clements, enthusiastically encouraged him.

After high school, Leo served in the Navy for three years. When he returned to New York, he studied at two of the finest art schools in the country. He attended the

Parsons School of Design and the School of the Visual Arts.

While studying at Parsons, Leo met Diane Sorber. She would become his wife and partner in the creation of some of the finest children's books of the past 40 years.

DIANE DILLON WAS BORN on March 13, 1933, in Glendale, California. "Dillon" became her last name when she got married. Her name when she was born was Diane Claire Sorber. Her parents were Adelbert and Phyllis Sorber. Adelbert was a teacher and Phyllis was a pianist.

DIANE DILLON GREW UP in the Los Angeles area. Like Leo, she loved to draw. "As a child, I drew all the time," she recalls. "My parents encouraged me, especially my father." Her Dad was a draftsman and artist. He helped her in whatever way he could.

DIANE DILLON WENT TO SCHOOL at the public schools in Los Angeles. She went on to Los Angeles City College in 1951. She studied art and planned to become a commercial artist.

But at the age of 18, Diane came down with tuberculosis (TB). TB is a very serious disease that destroys the lungs. It's treated with antibiotics now, but when Diane

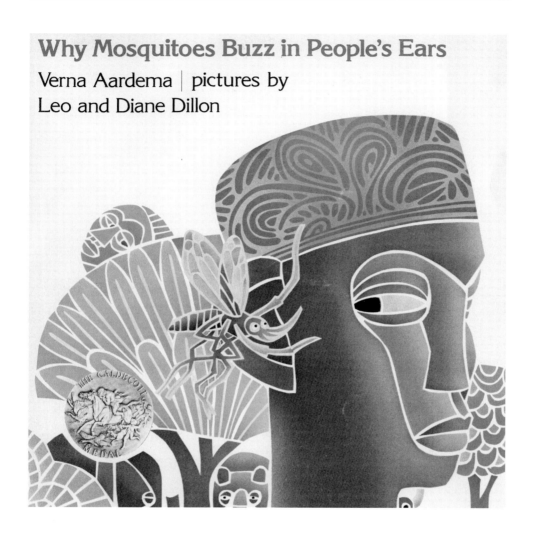

Why Mosquitoes Buzz in People's Ears
Verna Aardema | pictures by
Leo and Diane Dillon

got sick the only treatment was complete rest. She spent
the next year in a sanitarium, a kind of hospital. She was
able to continue to draw, though. When she was better,
she transferred to Skidmore College in New York.

Diane studied art at Skidmore for two years. But
because it is a liberal arts college, she had taken all the
art courses offered by Skidmore in just two years. She

decided to transfer to Parsons so she could focus on the subject she loved.

At Parsons, Diane met Leo Dillon. They admired each other's work right away. And right away, they became fiercely competitive. They recognized each other's talent, and, through competition, they learned from each other.

Soon, that competition led to friendship, and to love. They decided to keep their relationship private. In the 1950s, many Americans still held racist ideas. Interracial couples were sometimes harassed, even beaten. But Diane and Leo stayed together and married in 1957.

FIRST JOBS: Leo and Diane both started their careers in commercial art. Diane worked for an advertising firm, and Leo worked for a publishing company. After their marriage, Diane decided to stay home and try being a housewife. But she missed her work.

Sometimes, Leo brought home something he was working on. "He encouraged me to work with him on design problems, Diane recalls. "That was the beginning of our working together as one artist."

The Dillons decided to start their own commercial design company. They called it Studio 2. From the beginning, they liked to work in a wide variety of styles. They

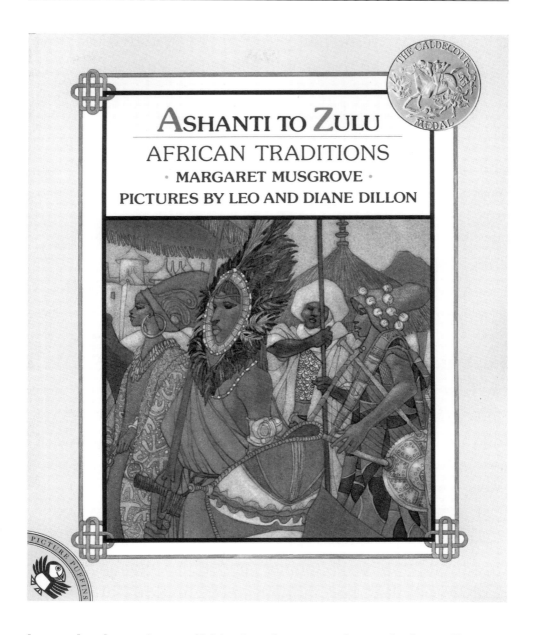

branched out into all kinds of art work, including illustration, album covers, and posters.

"We've never specialized," claims Diane. "At the very beginning we had trouble with that. Art directors kept telling us we had too many styles. They needed to know a specific style so they could remember us."

In 1959, the Dillons met sci-fi author Harlan Ellison. The began to produce illustrations for science fiction and fantasy works. These included many well-known works, like C. S. Lewis's "Narnia" books.

Since then, they've gone on to illustrate more than 40 books together. Some of the best-known and best-loved include *Why Mosquitos Buzz in People's Ears, Ashanti to Zulu,* and *The People Could Fly.*

WHY MOSQUITOES BUZZ IN PEOPLE'S EARS: In 1975, the Dillons created the illustrations for *Why Mosquitoes Buzz in People's Ears.* It's a retelling of a West African folktale, as retold by Verna Aardema. It tells the story of a pesky mosquito, and the mischief he makes for the creatures of the forest.

The Dillons' illustrations perfectly suit the text of this old folktale. Each animal—mosquito, iguana, python, rabbit, crow, monkey, owl, and lion—are recreated in rich color.

CALDECOTT MEDAL: The Dillon's art work won the book the Caldecott Medal in 1976. That is the highest award in children's book illustration. Leo was the first black artist to win a Caldecott Medal.

ASHANTI TO ZULU: The Dillons followed up their early success with another great book. *Ashanti to Zulu: African Traditions* was published in 1976. It's an alphabet book featuring 26 different African tribes. The book is beautifully illustrated, and makes learning about different African traditions a joy.

The Dillons won their second Caldecott Medal for *Ashanti to Zulu.* They are the only illustrators to ever win the award twice in a row.

THE PEOPLE COULD FLY: Another favorite book illustrated by the Dillons is *The People Could Fly.* It's a collection of folktales written by Virginia Hamilton. The tales are based on the lives of African-American slaves. Slaves used folktales to pass on their knowledge and their heritage. The tales are funny, and they are sad, too. Some tell of slavery itself. In "The People Could Fly," slaves fly away from their cruel master. The old slave Toby, as if by magic, murmurs the words that let them fly to freedom. The Dillons' illustrations capture the wondrous moments of these tales beautifully.

ILLUSTRATING FOR MANY AUTHORS: Over the years, the Dillons have illustrated for many of the best-loved children's authors. They illustrated several of Virginia Hamilton's books, and also those of Nancy Willard (*Pish Posh, Said Hieronymus Bosch*). The Dillons illustrated *Two Little Trains* by Margaret Wise Brown and *The Tale of the Mandarin Duck* by Katherine Paterson. They even illustrated a book by famous

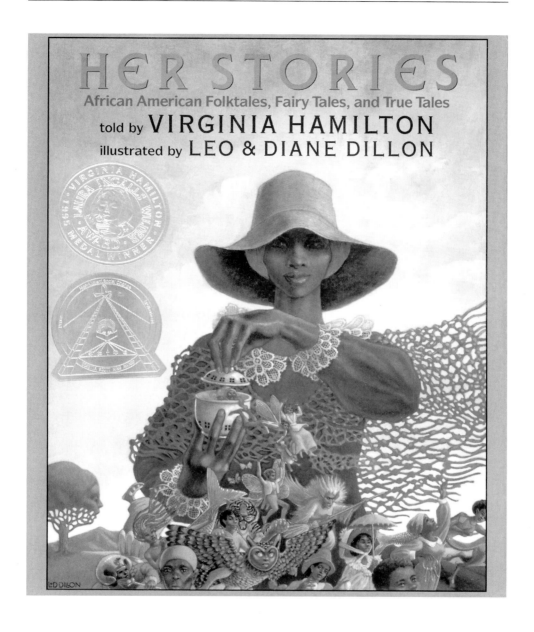

opera singer Leontyne Price, *Aida,* based on a famous opera by Verdi.

RAP A TAP TAP: Recently, the Dillons published a book they both wrote and illustrated. *Rap a Tap Tap:*

Here's Bojangles—Think of That! is about the life of the famous African-American tap dancer Bill "Bojangles" Robinson.

WORKING TOGETHER: Every piece of artwork that Leo and Diane Dillon create they do together. It's an unusual process. One of them sketches out an idea. Then they pass the piece back and forth, over and over. Each one adds to the work in progress, until they agree that it's finished.

The Dillons call their method the work of a "Third Artist." "The 'Third Artist' concept helped us a lot," says Diane. "We could look at ourselves as one artist rather than two individuals. That third artist was doing something neither one of us would do. That lifted the work away from reflecting either one's personal viewpoint. We let it flow the way it flows when artists work by themselves. A color goes down that they didn't quite expect and that affects the next colors they use, and it seems to have a life of its own."

"I'm constantly surprised at how our work is melding more and more as the years go by," says Leo. "In the beginning it was a conceived plan for us to work in a particular style, which we both could master. So in reality we were both working for 'someone else': the style. Forty years ago there were techniques neither one of us would attempt. Somewhere along the line, one picked it up and the other followed, and back and forth. For us to be able to collaborate is somewhat of an amazing thing."

The Dillons' illustrations have won numerous awards. In addition to their two Caldecott Medals, they have won several Coretta Scott King Awards. *Horn Book* magazine has honored their work, too.

RECENT BOOKS: The year 2007 marks the 50th year of partnership between these two great artists. They still have ideas for books and hope to work together for many years to come. In all their work, they strive to deliver an important message. "We all have a lot in common. It is our beliefs that divide us. We have little control over what life brings us, but we can change our thoughts."

"Art in its many forms has survived to inform us of lives long gone. Art inspires, lifts our spirits, and brings beauty to our lives. We wish to pay homage to it and the people who created it."

LEO AND DIANE DILLON'S HOME AND FAMILY: The Dillons still live in New York. They have one son, Lee, who was born in 1965. Lee is an artist, sculptor, and jewelry designer. He's also collaborated with his famous parents on illustrations and other works of art. He worked with them on the illustrations for Nancy Willard's *Pish Posh, Said Hieronymus Bosch.*

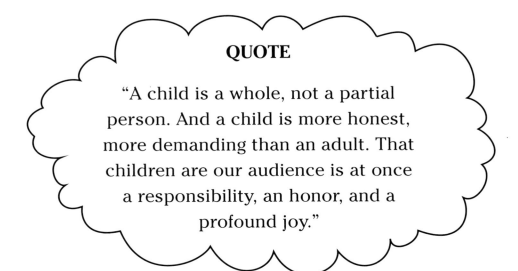

QUOTE

"A child is a whole, not a partial person. And a child is more honest, more demanding than an adult. That children are our audience is at once a responsibility, an honor, and a profound joy."

SOME OF LEO AND DIANE DILLON'S BOOKS:

As Illustrators:

The Ring and the Prairie

Burning Star

The Third Gift

Whirlwind Is a Ghost Dancing

Why Mosquitoes Buzz in People's Ears: A West African Tale

Ashanti to Zulu: African Traditions

Who's in Rabbit's House

Honey, I Love: and Other Love Poems

Tales from Scandinavia

Two Pairs of Shoes

Listen Children: An Anthology of Black Literature

Brother to the Wind

The People Could Fly: American Black Folktales

Moses' Ark: Stories from the Bible

Aida: A Picture Book for All Ages

The Race of the Golden Apples

Pish Posh, Said Hieronymus Bosch

Northern Lullaby

Many Thousand Gone: African Americans from Slavery to Freedom

What Am I? Looking through Shapes at Apples and Grapes

Her Stories: African American Folktales, Fairy Tales, and True Tales

The Girl Who Dreamed Only of Geese, and Other Tales of the Far North

To Everything There Is a Season

Wind Child

Mansa Musa: The Lion of the Mali

20,000 Leagues Under the Sea

The Girl Who Spun Gold

Two Little Trains

As Authors and Illustrators:

Rap a Tap Tap: Here's Bojangles, Think of That!

FOR MORE INFORMATION ABOUT LEO AND DIANE DILLON:

Write: HarperCollins Children's Books
       1350 Avenue of the Americas
       New York, NY 10019

WORLD WIDE WEB SITES:

http://www.childrenslit.com/l_dillons.html

http://www.embracingthechild.org/adillon.htm

http://www.harcourtbooks.com/AuthorInterviews/

http://www.kidsreads.com/authors/au-dillon-leo-diane.
  asp

http://www.locusmag.com/2000/Issues/04/Dillons.html

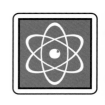

Hawking and his daughter, Lucy

Stephen Hawking
1942-
English Physicist and Writer
Co-Author of
George's Secret Key to the Universe

STEPHEN HAWKING WAS BORN on January 8, 1942, in Oxford, England. His birthday fell on the 300th anniversary of the death of Galileo Galilei, the famous Italian astronomer, physicist, and mathematician. Hawking's full name is Stephen William Hawking. His parents were Frank and Isobel Hawking. Frank was a doctor who did medical research about tropical diseases. Stephen was the oldest of four children in his family. He had two younger sisters, Mary and Philippa, and an adopted younger brother, Edward.

STEPHEN HAWKING GREW UP in a lively household where he was challenged to think about complex problems. The Hawkings lived in Highgate, a suburb of London, until Stephen was eight years old. In 1950 they moved to St. Albans, a village about 20 miles northwest of London.

STEPHEN HAWKING WENT TO SCHOOL at the highly competitive, all-boys St. Albans School. He remembers being skinny, uncoordinated, and somewhat nerdy as a boy. He was an average student until he focused on subjects he liked, like math and science. Then he found that he could get top grades without studying.

Hawking earned an honors degree from St. Albans School in 1962. He went on to Cambridge University, where he studied cosmology (the nature of the universe). He completed his doctoral degree at Cambridge in 1965.

LIVING WITH ALS: Hawking began having health problems during his time as a student at Cambridge. He often felt weak and fell down. In 1963 doctors diagnosed his condition as amyotrophic lateral sclerosis (ALS). It is also known as Lou Gehrig's disease, after a famous American baseball player who died from it. ALS affects

Hawking receives the Copley Medal,
the world's oldest scientific award.

the spinal cord and nerves. It causes people to lose the ability to control the movement of their muscles. There is no cure for ALS. People with ALS usually grow very weak, become paralyzed (unable to move), and die within a few years.

When Hawking first learned that he had ALS, he became very depressed. He worried that he would not live long enough to earn his degree from Cambridge. But his disease progressed much more slowly than expected.

He decided to live as fully as possible during whatever time he had left. "Although there was a cloud hanging over my future, I found, to my surprise, that I was enjoying life in the present more than before," he remembered.

In 1965 Hawking married Jane Wilde. His wife was able to care for him without outside help for the next ten years. Then they got part-time help from student assistants and visiting nurses. In 1985 Hawking caught pneumonia, a virus that attacks the lungs. He had so much trouble breathing that doctors had to use surgery to open a hole in his throat. The operation saved his life but left him unable to speak. From that time on, Hawking has needed full-time, live-in nursing care.

As of 2007, Hawking is almost completely paralyzed. He can only move one finger and some muscles in his right cheek. He uses his finger to drive a battery-powered wheelchair. He twitches his cheek to operate a special computer attached to the wheelchair. This computer allows Hawking to choose words and phrases from a database and put them together in sentences. He uses it to write books, speeches, and letters. He also sends the words to a speech synthesizer, which says them out loud in an electronic voice.

THEORIES ABOUT THE UNIVERSE: After completing his education at Cambridge, Hawking began working as

*Floating in space: Hawking experiences
weightlessness during a zero-gravity flight.*

a theoretical physicist. He came up with new ideas, or
"theories," to explain the basic laws controlling the universe. Since the universe is so big, Hawking could not
use regular scientific experiments to test his theories.
Instead, he used complicated mathematical formulas to
prove his ideas.

BLACK HOLES: One subject of Hawking's research was
"black holes." Black holes are features of the universe
that have such intense gravity that they pull in everything around them. For many years, scientists believed
that nothing could escape a black hole—not even light.

Around 1970 Hawking discovered a new property of black holes. He found that they gave off radiation, or energy. His discovery challenged the belief that nothing could escape from a black hole. Scientists now use the term "Hawking radiation" to describe the energy that comes out of black holes.

For much of his career, Hawking believed that anything pulled into a black hole would disappear without a trace. But in 2004 he announced a new discovery. He showed that black holes actually preserve information about the objects they swallow up. The information gets all mixed up, but it continues to exist.

After announcing his findings, Hawking was forced to pay off a bet he had made 30 years earlier. He sent a baseball encyclopedia to the American astrophysicist John Preskill. Preskill had always said that black holes must preserve information about the objects they pull in.

Hawking also developed important theories about the origin of the universe. Many scientists believe that the universe got started suddenly through a huge explosion. This idea is known as the "big bang theory." Hawking questioned the big bang theory. He suggested that the universe did not begin with a specific event. Instead, he claimed that it was in a constant state of change, with no beginning or end.

EXPLAINING SCIENCE: Hawking always felt that it was important for ordinary people to understand the basic laws of the universe. He tried to explain some of his theories in popular books and television series.

In 1988 Hawking published *A Brief History of Time: From the Big Bang to Black Holes.* This book explains major theories about the universe in simple terms. It sold 10 million copies and made Hawking the best-known scientist in the world. In 1992 the book was turned into a movie. The movie version included lots of added information about Hawking's life and work.

Hawking appeared in a six-part PBS television series called *Stephen Hawking's Universe* in 1997. He also became a guest star on several TV shows, including *Star Trek: The Next Generation* and *The Simpsons.*

In 2002 Hawking published *The Universe in a Nutshell.* This book provides young adult readers with a brief introduction to his theories. Three years later Hawking published *A Briefer History of Time,* a shorter and clearer version of his earlier book.

Hawking published his first children's book, *George's Secret Key to the Universe,* in 2007. He wrote it with his daughter, Lucy. It tells the story of a boy who goes on an exciting voyage through the universe with a scientist and his daughter. Hawking hopes that the book will help make science more interesting and understandable for students in elementary school.

A CELEBRITY SCIENTIST: Many people say that Hawking is the world's most famous living scientist. He has won countless awards for his brilliant theories. In 1974 he became one of the youngest people ever admitted to the Royal Society. This group includes all of the leading scientists in England. In 1979 he was appointed as the Lucasian Professor of Mathematics at Cambridge. This special post was once held by the famous mathematician and physicist Isaac Newton.

Hawking's books have helped ordinary people understand complex scientific ideas. But Hawking is probably best known for his courage in facing extreme disability.

Hawking has lived with ALS for more than 40 years. He has refused to let the disease stop him from doing important work in physics. In fact, thinking about the laws of the universe has helped him put his disability in perspective. "The human race is so puny compared to the universe that being disabled is not of much cosmic significance," he stated.

In 2007 Hawking became the first person with a disability to experience a zero-gravity flight. He was a passenger on a special jet plane that repeatedly climbed to a high altitude, then plunged back toward Earth. Every time the plane reached the top of a climb, the passengers felt weightless for 25 seconds.

Hawking enjoyed the feeling of floating around like an astronaut. He also used the flight as a way to bring attention to worldwide problems. He warned that global climate change and nuclear weapons threaten to end human survival on the planet. "I think the human race has no future if it doesn't go into space," he explained.

STEPHEN HAWKING'S HOME AND FAMILY: Hawking married his first wife, Jane Wilde, in 1965. They had three children together: Robert, Timothy, and Lucy. Hawking and his first wife separated in 1990 and eventually divorced. In 1995 he married his former nurse, Elaine Mason. They separated in early 2007. Hawking lives in a large house in Newnham, one of the fancier neighborhoods of Cambridge.

QUOTE

"My goal is simple. It is complete understanding of the universe, why it is as it is and why it exists at all."

FOR MORE INFORMATION ABOUT STEPHEN HAWKING:

WORLD WIDE WEB SITES:

http://www.hawking.org.uk

http://news.bbc.co.uk/2/hi/science/nature/1746912.stm

http://www.pbs.org/wgbh/aso/databank/entries/bphawk.
html

LeBron James
1984-
American Professional Basketball Player
with the Cleveland Cavaliers

LEBRON JAMES WAS BORN on December 30, 1984, in Akron, Ohio. His mother is Gloria James. She had LeBron when she was just 16 years old and raised him as a single mom. His biological father has never been part of his life.

LEBRON JAMES GREW UP in Akron in a number of different places. His Mom had a hard time making ends meet. She switched jobs often, and LeBron moved seven times by the age of five. Sometimes, she couldn't care for him. He lived with a foster family for two years.

LEBRON JAMES WENT TO SCHOOL at the local elementary schools wherever he lived. Because he moved so often, he missed a lot of school. But then he discovered basketball. It became an important force in his life. It gave him focus and stability.

LeBron and his mom actually lived for awhile with his coach, Frankie Walker. Under Walker's coaching, LeBron became a great player. He played with an amateur athletic team that made the national finals when he was 13.

By the time LeBron was in high school, he was getting noticed. He attended St. Vincent-St. Mary High School in Akron, where he studied hard and became a basketball star.

HIGH SCHOOL BASKETBALL: James was a standout player from his freshman year. That first year, he led the team to the Ohio state finals. He repeated that feat the next year. When he was a junior, James brought the team to the finals again. And every year, his own stats got better and better. He averaged 18 points a game as a freshman, 26 points as a sophomore, and 29 points as a junior.

James has always been known for his team play, and his stats from high school prove it. In addition to being a top scorer, he could rebound, assist, and steal the ball, too.

By the time LeBron was a senior, he was a national star. His high school games were being broadcast on national TV. He was known around the country as one of the nation's best players.

All the attention caused some problems for LeBron and his family. His Mom borrowed a lot of money to buy him a fancy car. She and her boyfriend borrowed money to try to win LeBron endorsement contracts. And LeBron accepted two valuable NBA jerseys.

There are strict rules about what gifts non-pro athletes can accept. As a high school student, LeBron shouldn't have accepted the jerseys. He gave them back, but since he'd broken a rule, he had to sit out one game.

His problems didn't effect his playing, though. As a senior, James led his team to the Ohio state championships once again. With LeBron bringing in crowds, the games had to be played at college arenas.

The team, and LeBron, won national honors that year, too. The team was named the best in the nation by

James battles under the boards.

USA Today. Several groups named him MVP (Most Valuable Player) of the year.

In the spring of 2003, James decided he wanted to join the NBA (National Basketball Association). Most players go to college first, but James thought he was ready for the pros. His success over the last four years has proved him right.

JOINING THE NBA: James was picked first in the NBA draft of 2003. That is a great honor, and usually goes to the finest college player. But the high school player was the Number 1 pick of the Cleveland Cavaliers. Fans everywhere were eager to watch the young star.

STAR OF THE CLEVELAND CAVALIERS: From his very first game with the Cavs, James showed his star power. In his first season, he became the youngest player ever to score 40 points in a game. That year, he averaged 20.9 points, 5.5 rebounds, and 5.9 assists per game.

In the 2004-2005 season, James raised the level of his play even higher. That season, he averaged 27 points, 7.4 rebounds, and 7.2 assists. The 2005-2006 season ended with the Cavs battling the Detroit Pistons for the Eastern finals. The Pistons held them off, with James playing great ball.

James in a playoff game against the Detroit Pistons.

James in an ad for Bubblicious gum.

James was in great shape again for the 2006-2007 season. Averaging 27.3 points per game, with 6.7 rebounds and 6 assists, he led his team to the conference finals again. Once again, they met the Pistons. But this time, James played some of the best basketball of his life. Against a team of NBA veterans, he led his team to victory over the Pistons and to the NBA finals. It was the first time the Cavaliers had ever gone to the championships.

THE 2007 NBA FINALS: James and the Cavaliers faced the San Antonio Spurs in the finals. The Spurs have won the championship three times in the last five years. They're a team of powerful players, with plenty of speed and strength. The series went four games, with James playing as hard as he could. But it wasn't enough, and the Spurs emerged the winners.

It was still an awesome feat for the Cavs to make it to the finals. And James shone as their star player. Many believe that Cleveland will be back to the finals soon. Much of their strength will come from a man known for his unselfish play.

From the beginning of his pro career, James has been a team player. He values his teammates, and they value him, too. "When he gets the ball, you better have your hands up and ready because he's going to find you," says teammate Carlos Boozer.

The fans love James, too. He's made the All-Star team three times, in 2005, 2006, and 2007.

FUTURE PLANS: James just wants to keep playing, and getting better and better. Many in the sports world think he may become the best player in basketball history. They compare him to Michael Jordan, and think LeBron may break all of Michael's records. But James stays humble. He sees basketball as a team sport, and he wants to lead his team to championships.

LEBRON JAMES'S HOME AND FAMILY: James has two sons with his girlfriend, Savannah Brinson. LeBron Jr. was born in 2004, and Bryce was born in June 2007, right in the middle of the NBA finals. James is building a huge house outside Akron for his growing family. He's still very close to his mom, Gloria.

James makes millions of dollars a year, as a player, and also endorsing products. He's in ads for Nike, Bubblicious gum, Powerade, and other items. He's happy to share his good fortune with those less fortunate, too. He's formed a foundation that helps poor kids in the Cleveland area.

QUOTE

"Working with all of these kids is great. It doesn't get any better than this, to come down and inspire kids who want to play the game of basketball and put smiles on their faces."

FOR MORE INFORMATION ABOUT LEBRON JAMES:

Write: The Cleveland Cavaliers
One Center Court
Cleveland, OH 44115

WORLD WIDE WEB SITES:

http://www.lebronjames.com

http://www.nba.com.playerfile/lebron_james/index.html

Richard Peck

1934-
American Author
for Children and Young Adults
Creator of *A Long Way from Chicago*
and *A Year Down Yonder*

RICHARD PECK WAS BORN on April 5, 1934, in Decatur, Illinois. His parents were Wayne and Virginia Peck. Wayne owned a gas station and Virginia was a dietician.

RICHARD PECK GREW UP in Decatur. It was a Midwestern town, where the neighbors knew each other, and what their kids were up to. He also grew up with a mom who loved to read to him. "My mother read to me, making me hungry for books and school and the world," he recalled. "Because of this, I wanted to be a writer before I could read."

RICHARD PECK WENT TO SCHOOL at the local public schools in Decatur. At that time, most schools were segregated by race. But in Decatur, Peck went to school with kids from all backgrounds, rich and poor, black and white.

Peck did well in school, and after high school went to college at DePauw University in Indiana. He spent his junior year in England, at the University of Exeter. It was a wonderful experience.

After Peck graduated from college in 1956, he was drafted into the Army. He spent the next two years in Germany. There, he worked for an Army chaplain. He often wrote sermons for the chaplain (without getting credit for it).

Peck returned to Illinois and worked on a master's degree in English. After completing his master's, he got a teaching job. Even though he wanted to be a writer, he thought teaching was a "safer" way to make a living. "In Decatur we'd been brought up to make a living and not to take chances. So I became an English teacher, thinking

this was as close to the written word as I'd be allowed to come."

FIRST JOBS: Peck taught English at Glenbrook North High School, near Chicago. That's where he first got the inspiration to write. "Teaching made a writer out of me," he claimed. "It was in teaching that I found my readers." He worked there for a few years, then got a job in New York.

Peck moved to New York City, and taught English for several years. But in 1971, he decided to leave teaching behind. He quit his job and started to write.

It was scary, but it offered him freedom. "I wrote my first line of fiction on May 24th, 1971," he recalls. "I'd quit my teaching job that day."

STARTING TO WRITE FOR KIDS: Peck knew what he wanted to say, and who he was writing for. "I wrote with my own students in mind," he recalled.

"A novel is about the individual within the group," he says. "That's how I saw young people every day, as their parents never do. In all my novels, you have to declare your independence from your peers before you can take that first step toward yourself."

Peck found an editor who liked his first novel. It was published in 1971, and he was on his way. He's been able to make his living as a writer ever since.

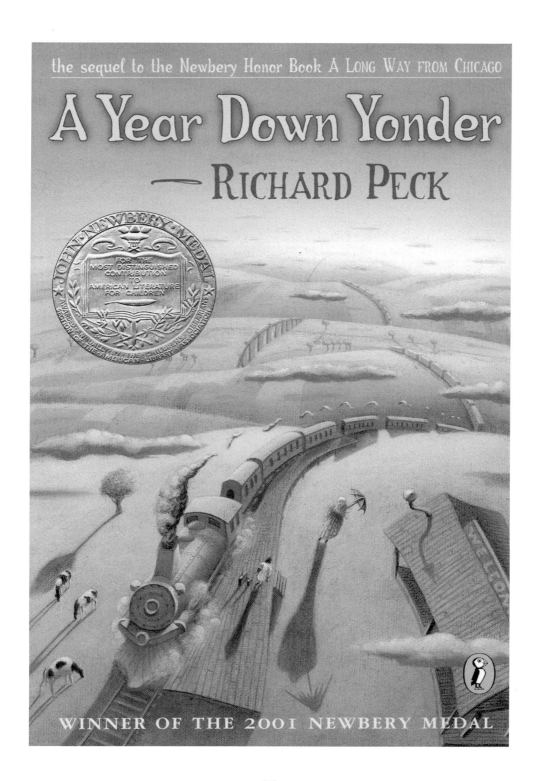

Peck's first books covered the problems teens face growing up. Those early books are mostly for, and about, young adults. Over the years Peck's audience has grown. Now he writes books beloved by readers who range in age from elementary school students to adults. Three recent favorites include *A Long Way from Chicago, A Year Down Yonder,* and *Here Lies the Librarian.*

A LONG WAY FROM CHICAGO: *A Long Way From Chicago* features one of Peck's most-beloved characters, Grandma Dowdel. She's not your "regular" grandma. To her grandchildren, Joey and Mary Alice, Grandma Dowdel is a wonder. "What little we knew about grown-ups didn't seem to cover Grandma," Joey recalls. This novel is actually seven stories. Woven together, they give a warm, funny look into the seven summers that Joey and Mary Alice spend with their grandma.

The novel takes place during the Depression. That was a time in the 1930s when many Americans lost their jobs and money was tight. Peck doesn't shy away from showing how tough times were then. But all the stories shine with the love and humor of a close family. The novel won Peck a Newbery Honor.

A YEAR DOWN YONDER: *A Year Down Yonder* is a sequel to *A Long Way from Chicago.* Grandma Dowdel is again the feisty central character. But this time, the

RICHARD PECK

Newbery-winning author of **A YEAR DOWN YONDER**

Here Lies
the Librarian

SHH!

story is told through the eyes of Mary Alice. She's now 15, and has been sent to live with her grandma because her dad has lost his job. Mary Alice hates leaving Chicago for the "hick town" in Southern Illinois. But she slowly learns to love her new town, and her place in it.

A Year Down Yonder won Peck a Newbery Medal. That's the highest honor in children's books. He was delighted, and surprised, by the award.

HERE LIES THE LIBRARIAN: Another recent favorite is *Here Lies the Librarian.* It features a spunky heroine named Eleanor McGrath. "Peewee," as she's called, runs a car shop with her brother, Jake. The novel is set in 1914, in rural Indiana.

Peewee's an independent girl, and a tomboy. She loves cars, and she thinks that a traditional "woman's life" is not for her. Then several young women hit town. They are librarians who show Peewee what it *really* means to be a woman. The book was a great hit with young readers, and quite a few librarians, too.

RICHARD PECK'S HOME AND FAMILY: Peck, who never married, lives in New York City. He lives in an apartment, where he works at a desk without a computer. Instead, Peck is devoted to an old typewriter.

Peck also travels all over the country, meeting his many fans. They're still his inspiration. "I now travel about 60,000 miles a year, on the trail of the young. Now, I never start a novel until some young reader, somewhere, gives me the necessary nudge."

SOME OF RICHARD PECK'S BOOKS:

A Long Way from Chicago

A Year Down Yonder

Fair Weather

Here Lies the Librarian

The River Between Us

On the Wings of Heroes

FOR MORE INFORMATION ABOUT RICHARD PECK:

Write: Dial Books for Young Readers
375 Hudson St.
New York, NY 10014

WORLD WIDE WEB SITES:

http://cbcbooks.org/cbcmagazine/meet/richard_peck.
html

http://eduscapes.com/newbery/

http://embracingthechild.org/apeck.html

http://www.randomhouse.com/author/

http://www.scholastic.com/

http://us.penguingroup.com/nf/Author

Peck believes passionately in the importance of parents reading to their kids. Here's a poem he wrote about it:

QUOTE

Twenty Minutes a Day

Read to your children
Twenty minutes a day.
You have the time,
And so do they.
Read while the laundry is in the machine,
Read while the dinner cooks,
Tuck a child in the crook of your arm
And reach for the library books.
Hide the remote,
Let the computer games cool,
For one day your children will be off to school.
Remedial? Gifted? You have the choice.
Let them hear their first tales
In the sound of your voice.
Read in the morning,
Read over noon.
Read by the light of
"Goodnight Moon."
Turn the page together,
Sitting close as you'll fit,
Till a small voice beside you says,
"Hey, don't quit."

J.K. Rowling
1965-
English Author
Creator of the *Harry Potter* Series

[***Editor's Note:*** *In honor of the final volume of the* Harry Potter *series, we are presenting this updated version of the J.K. Rowling sketch. She originally appeared in the Fall 2000 issue of* Biography for Beginners.]

J.K. ROWLING WAS BORN on July 31, 1965, in Chipping Sodbury, near Bristol, England. Her full name is Joanne Kathleen Rowling. Her last name is pronounced "rolling." Her parents were Peter and Ann Rowling. Peter managed an aircraft factory, and Ann was a lab technician. Rowling has one sister, Diane.

J.K. ROWLING GREW UP in the town of Winterbourne in southern England. As a child, she loved to make up stories. When she was only six, she knew she wanted to be a writer. She also used to play with the neighborhood kids. Two neighbors had the last name of "Potter," a name she would use later in her famous books.

When she was nine, Rowling and her family moved to Tutshill, in Wales. It was out in the country, and they all loved it. She and her sister wandered for hours "across fields and along the river."

J.K. ROWLING WENT TO SCHOOL at the local schools in Winterbourne and Tutshill. When she moved to Tutshill, she remembers being treated badly at school. She took a math test that included fractions. She had never learned how to do them, so she flunked the test. The teacher put her on the right side of the room. Later, it became clear to her that she was, in her words, "in the 'stupid' row." She felt ashamed, and she never forgot.

Despite her early problems, Rowling did well in school. She loved English and languages especially. She continued to write stories. Sometimes, she'd share

these tales with friends at lunch. The stories featured her friends, "doing heroic and daring deeds we certainly wouldn't have done in real life," she recalls.

When Rowling was a teenager, her mother became ill with multiple sclerosis (M.S.). M.S. is a disease of the nervous system. Her mother died of the disease in 1990. It was a time of great tragedy for the family.

After graduating from Wyedean Comprehensive School (high school), Rowling went to college. She attended Exeter University and studied French.

FIRST JOBS: After graduating from college, Rowling worked as a secretary. She was horrible at it. She claims that she was "the worst secretary ever." She used most of her time to "type up stories on the computer when no one was looking." In 1990, she left that job and moved to Portugal.

Portugal was Rowling's home for the next three years. She taught English to Portuguese students. She also had free time to write. It was during those years that she created the character that made her famous.

CREATING HARRY POTTER: Rowling says she was riding on a train in England when the idea of Harry Potter came to her. She was "staring out the window at some cows, thinking of nothing in particular," she says. Then, "the idea for Harry just kind of fell into my head." Over the next few months, she began to write the story down.

Then things began to fall apart in her personal life. She had married a Portuguese journalist and had a baby, Jessica. The marriage ended. Rowling was a broke, single mother.

She moved to Edinburgh, Scotland, to live near her sister. With an infant to care for and no job, Rowling went on welfare. She remembers feeling shame and anger. She didn't have money for child care, so she couldn't work.

"It's the most soul-destroying thing," Rowling says about being poor. "We were quite broke. But we weren't starving. A couple of times I did skip meals."

Rowling knew she needed to get back to her Harry Potter story. She made a friend at church who offered to sit for Jessica. Rowling started to write in coffee shops all over town. She'd write by herself, and sometimes take Jessica. She found places that let her "sit for two hours while my daughter napped, over one cold cup of coffee."

Rowling says the book "saved my sanity." She was proud of herself, too. "It was proof positive of how much I wanted to write about Harry," she says.

When the book was done, she tried to find a publisher. She received many rejections, but finally Bloomsbury publishers bought the book. *Harry Potter and the Sorcerer's Stone* was published in Britain in 1997. It was an immediate hit.

HARRY POTTER AND THE SORCERER'S STONE: The first book begins on the eve of Harry Potter's 11th birthday. He is living with his miserably cruel aunt, uncle, and cousin. Harry is an orphan. Soon, he learns that his parents had been famous wizards.

Harry is visited by a giant, Hagrid. He takes Harry away from the world of humans—"muggles." They go to Hogwarts School of Witchcraft and Wizardry. There, Harry learns more about his parents and his own true nature.

Harry Potter and the Sorcerer's Stone takes place in the magical world of Hogwarts. Harry meets his fellow students. Some are kind and become good friends. Some are cruel and prove to be enemies.

Harry takes courses in how to cast spells and use magic wands. He learns to play the marvelous game of

Quidditch. It's kind of like soccer, but played in the air on broomsticks with live balls.

Harry also learns about the evil Voldemort. He is a powerful wizard so evil that students won't say his name. He is also responsible for the death of Harry's parents.

In the book, Harry and his friends search for the sorcerer's stone, a magical stone of great power. The story is fast-paced, funny, and suspenseful. Readers of all ages loved the book. It was a bestseller all over the world. Harry's eager fans wanted more.

HARRY POTTER AND THE CHAMBER OF SECRETS: Rowling published her second book about Harry in 1999. In _Harry Potter and the Chamber of Secrets_ the setting is Hogwarts again. It is Harry's second year at the school. This time, he and his friends must find an evil monster that is turning students to stone.

Once again, Harry must face the evil Voldemort. He notices that his own powers as a wizard are growing. He learns he has to use them only for good. And he has to

deal with his cruel enemy, Draco Malfoy, on and off the Quidditch field.

The story is filled with the same action, adventure, and thrills that made the first book so popular. It was an instant success in the U.S. and Britain.

HARRY POTTER AND THE PRISONER OF AZKABAN:

Rowling's next Harry book came out in the summer of 1999. *Harry Potter and the Prisoner of Azkaban* takes place during Harry's third year at Hogwarts. In this book, Harry must deal with the mysterious Sirius Black. Black is connected to Voldemort and to his parents' death. Now he is stalking Harry.

The book, like the first two, was an instant success. It came out in Britain on July 8, 1999, at 3:45p.m. British kids go to school in the summer. The British publisher knew that kids would want the book immediately. They released it after school got out for the day, so kids wouldn't skip school to buy it.

In the U.S., Harry Potter lovers couldn't wait for the American release, set for late September. They ordered the British version over the Internet. That caused the U.S. publisher to move up the U.S. publication date. Once again, Rowling and Harry were a tremendous hit. The books sold millions of copies, and fans read the first three books over and over, while they waited for Number Four.

HARRY POTTER AND THE GOBLET OF FIRE: On July 8, 2000, fans all over the world thrilled to the new adventures of Harry. *Harry Potter and the Goblet of Fire* was released at Midnight on July 8th, and many bookstores had parties to celebrate. Kids and adults dressed up as characters from the series. Some bookstores had cauldrons full of oatmeal, and live owls, in honor of the new book.

The Goblet of Fire features Harry in his fourth year at Hogwarts. The main event in the novel is a Triwizard competition that pits Harry against three other students from wizard schools around the world. The book was the longest to date—734 pages. But the length didn't keep readers from devouring it the first weekend it was available.

HARRY POTTER AND THE ORDER OF THE PHOENIX:
Rowling's fifth book about Harry, _Harry Potter and the Order of the Phoenix,_ appeared on June 21, 2003. It was the fastest-selling book in history, and once again Harry's many fans held parties at bookstores all over the world. The book had a distinctly darker quality, as it revealed the growing power of Voldemort.

HARRY POTTER AND THE HALF-BLOOD PRINCE:
Harry's sixth appearance broke all the records again. By the time _The Half-Blood Prince_ appeared on July 16, 2005, there were 10.2 million copies sold. In this book, Rowling reveals the mystery of Voldemort's past. And it ends with the tragic death of a beloved character.

HARRY POTTER AND THE DEATHLY HALLOWS: The _Harry Potter_ series came to a dramatic close on July 21, 2007. On that day, _Harry Potter and the Deathly Hallows_ appeared. Readers by the millions began devouring the last volume in the beloved series. For many, it was a time of great sadness. How could this great saga come to an end? But readers everywhere will continue to delight in the wonderful world Rowling first brought to life 10 years ago. For them, Harry, and the world of Hogwarts, will live forever.

ONE OF THE BEST-SELLING AUTHORS OF ALL TIME:
As Rowling retires the character that made her famous, she's sold over a quarter billion books. These beloved

Poster announcing the sixth volume in the series.

children's classics have been translated into over 60 languages. They are available in over 200 countries.

THE *HARRY POTTER* MOVIES: Each of the Harry Potter books has been, or will be, made into a movie. The films, too, have been fabulously successful. Audiences of all ages thrill to the adaptations, which have starred young actors Daniel Radcliffe and Emma Watson, as well as adult stars like Maggie Smith and Alan Rickman.

FUTURE PLANS: J.K. Rowling is now taking a well-deserved rest. She does have plans for new books, though. And she plans to write a kind of Harry Potter "encyclopedia." It will be full of information about Hogwarts and background stories of many characters from the books.

J.K. ROWLING'S HOME AND FAMILY: In 2001, Rowling married again. Her husband is named Dr. Neil Murray. Now the family has grown to include three children.

QUOTE

"I am an extraordinarily lucky person, doing what I love best in the world. I'm sure that I will always be a writer. It was wonderful enough just to be published. The greatest reward is the enthusiasm of the readers."

Jessica has a brother, David, and a sister, Mackenzie. The family lives in Scotland.

Rowling has always given generously to charities. She created two special books, *Quidditch through the Ages* and *Fantastic Beasts & Where to Find Them* to raise money for a foundation called "Harry's Book Fund." The money from the sales helps poor children around the world.

THE HARRY POTTER BOOKS:

Harry Potter and the Sorcerer's Stone, 1997
Harry Potter and the Chamber of Secrets, 1999
Harry Potter and the Prisoner of Azkaban, 1999
Harry Potter and the Goblet of Fire, 2000
Harry Potter and the Order of the Phoenix, 2003
Harry Potter and the Half-Blood Prince, 2005
Harry Potter and the Deathly Hallows, 2007

FOR MORE INFORMATION ABOUT J.K. ROWLING:

Write: Scholastic Inc.
557 Broadway
New York, NY 10012

WORLD WIDE WEB SITES:

http://www.bloomsbury.com
http://www.jkrowling.com
http://www.kidsreads.com/HP07/content/rowling.asp
http://www.scholastic.com/harrypotter

Name Index

Listed below are the names of all individuals who have appeared in *Biography for Beginners*, followed by the issue and year in which they appear.

Subject Index

This index includes subjects, occupations, and ethnic and minority origins for individuals who have appeared in *Biography for Beginners*.

Pinkwater, Daniel, Spring 2000

Polacco, Patricia, Fall '97

Potter, Beatrix, Fall '98

Prelutsky, Jack, Spring '95

Raschka, Chris, Spring 2006

Rey, H. A., Fall 2006

Rey, Margret, Fall 2006

Ringgold, Faith, Spring '99

Rohmann, Eric, Spring 2004

Rowling, J.K., Fall 2000, Fall 2007

Rylant, Cynthia, Fall '96

Sabuda, Robert, Spring 2005

Sachar, Louis, Spring 2002

Scarry, Richard, Spring '95

Scieszka, Jon, Fall '95

Sendak, Maurice, Spring '96

Seuss, Dr., Spring '95

Shannon, David, Fall 2006

Silverstein, Shel, Spring '97

Sis, Peter, Fall 2004

Small, David, Fall 2002

Steig, William, Spring 2000

Van Allsburg, Chris, Spring '96

Viorst, Judith, Fall 2006

Wells, Rosemary, Spring '96

White, E.B., Spring 2002

Wiesner, David, Spring 2007

Wilder, Laura Ingalls, Fall '96

Willard, Nancy, Spring 2004

Williams, Garth, Fall '96

Willems, Mo, Spring 2007

Wood, Audrey, Spring 2003

Wood, Don, Spring 2003

Yolen, Jane, Spring '99

autobiographer

Angelou, Maya, Fall 2006

baseball players

Bonds, Barry, Fall 2002

Griffey, Ken Jr., Fall '95

Jeter, Derek, Fall 2000

Martinez, Pedro, Spring 2001

McGwire, Mark, Spring '99

Ripken, Cal Jr., Fall '96

Sosa, Sammy, Spring '99

Suzuki, Ichiro, Fall 2003

basketball players

Bryant, Kobe, Fall '99

Vince, Fall 2001

MacLachlan, Patricia, Spring 2003

Martin, Ann M., Spring '96

McKissack, Patricia, Fall '98

Miller, Shannon, Spring '95

Moceanu, Dominique, Fall '98

Nechita, Alexandra, Spring 2000

Numeroff, Laura, Fall '99

Ochoa, Ellen, Spring 2005

O'Donnell, Rosie, Fall '99

Oleynik, Larisa, Spring '96

Olsen, Ashley, Spring '95

Olsen, Mary-Kate, Spring '95

Osborne, Mary Pope, Fall 2001

Parish, Peggy, Spring '97

Park, Barbara, Spring '98

Parks, Rosa, Fall '95

Paterson, Katherine, Spring 2007

Patrick, Danica, Fall 2005

Pinkney, Andrea Davis, Fall 2004

Polacco, Patricia, Fall '97

Potter, Beatrix, Fall '98

Raven, Spring 2004

Rey, Margret, Fall 2006

Rice, Condoleezza, Spring 2002

Ringgold, Faith, Spring '99

Rowling, J.K., Fall 2000; Revised, Fall 2007

Rylant, Cynthia, Fall '96

Scurry, Briana, Fall '99

Strug, Kerri, Spring '97

Swoopes, Sheryl, Spring 2000

Teresa, Mother, Fall '98

Van Dyken, Amy, Spring 2000

Viorst, Judith, Fall 2006

Watson, Emma, Fall 2004

Wells, Rosemary, Spring '96

Wie, Michelle, Spring 2004

Wilder, Laura Ingalls, Fall '96

Willard, Nancy, Spring 2004

Williams, Serena, Fall 2003

Wilson, Mara, Spring '97

Winfrey, Oprah, Fall 2002

Wood, Audrey, Spring 2003

Yamaguchi, Kristi, Fall '97

Yolen, Jane, Spring '99

film director

Parks, Gordon, Spring 2007

inventors

Swedish

Lindgren, Astrid, Fall 2002

swimmers

Phelps, Michael, Spring 2006

Van Dyken, Amy, Spring 2000

television

Allen, Tim, Fall '96

Brandy, Fall '96

Bryan, Zachery Ty, Spring '97

Burton, LeVar, Spring '98

Bynes, Amanda, Spring 2005

Cannon, Nick, Spring 2003

Couric, Katie, Spring 2007

Cyrus, Miley, Fall 2007

Duff, Hilary, Spring 2003

Efron, Zac, Fall 2006

Ellerbee, Linda, Fall 2003

Hart, Melissa Joan, Fall '95

Hudgens, Vanessa Anne, Spring 2007

Irwin, Steve, Spring 2003

Lewis, Shari, Spring '99

Muniz, Frankie, Fall 2001

Nye, Bill, Spring '99

O'Donnell, Rosie, Fall '99

Oleynik, Larisa, Spring '96

Olsen, Ashley, Spring '95

Olsen, Mary-Kate, Spring '95

Raven, Spring 2004

Rogers, Fred, Fall '98

Thomas, Jonathan Taylor, Fall '95

White, Jaleel, Fall '97

Winfrey, Oprah, Fall 2002

tennis

Williams, Serena, Fall 2003

United Nations

Annan, Kofi, Fall 2000

Vice President of the United States

Cheney, Dick, Fall 2003

Gore, Al, Fall '97

Birthday Index

January

7 Katie Couric (1957)
8 Stephen Hawking (1942)
12 John Lasseter (1957)
14 Shannon Lucid (1943)
17 Shari Lewis (1934)
21 Hakeem Olajuwon (1963)
26 Vince Carter (1977)
28 Wayne Gretzky (1961)
29 Bill Peet (1915)
Rosemary Wells (1943)
Oprah Winfrey (1954)
30 Dick Cheney (1941)
31 Bryan Collier (1967)

February

2 Judith Viorst (1931)
4 Rosa Parks (1913)
5 David Wiesner (1956)
7 Laura Ingalls Wilder (1867)
9 Wilson "Snowflake" Bentley (1865)
11 Jane Yolen (1939)
Brandy (1979)
12 Judy Blume (1938)
David Small (1945)
13 Mary GrandPré (1954)
15 Norman Bridwell (1928)
Amy Van Dyken (1973)
16 LeVar Burton (1957)
17 Michael Jordan (1963)
22 Steve Irwin (1962)
24 Steven Jobs (1955)
27 Chelsea Clinton (1980)

March

2 Leo Dillon (1933)
Dr. Seuss (1904)
David Satcher (1941)
3 Patricia MacLachlan (1938)
Jackie Joyner-Kersee (1962)
4 Garrett Morgan (1877)
Dav Pilkey (1966)
5 Mem Fox (1946)
Jake Lloyd (1989)
6 Chris Raschka (1959)
8 Robert Sabuda (1965)
10 Shannon Miller (1977)
11 Ezra Jack Keats (1916)
Virginia Hamilton (1936)
Diane Dillon (1933)

15 Ruth Bader Ginsburg (1933)

16 Shaquille O'Neal (1972)

17 Mia Hamm (1972)

18 Bonnie Blair (1964)

20 Fred Rogers (1928)
Lois Lowry (1937)
Louis Sachar (1954)

21 Rosie O'Donnell (1962)

25 DiCamillo, Kate (1964)
Sheryl Swoopes (1971)
Danica Patrick (1982)

31 Al Gore (1948)

April

3 Jane Goodall (1934)
Amanda Bynes (1986)

4 Maya Angelou (1928)

5 Richard Peck (1934)
Colin Powell (1937)
Dean Kamen (1951)

7 RondeBarber (1975)
Tiki Barber (1975)

8 Kofi Annan (1938)

12 Beverly Cleary (1916)
Tony Hawk (1968)

15 Tim Duncan (1976)
Emma Watson (1990)

16 Garth Williams (1912)

18 Melissa Joan Hart (1976)

26 Patricia Reilly Giff (1935)

27 Ludwig Bemelmans (1898)
Coretta Scott King (1927)
Barbara Park (1947)

May

4 Don Wood (1945)

6 Judy Delton (1931)
Ted Lewin (1935)

10 Leo Lionni (1910)
Christopher Paul Curtis (1953)
Ellen Ochoa (1958)

11 Peter Sis (1949)

12 Betsy Lewin (1937)

14 George Lucas (1944)
Emmitt Smith (1969)

16 Margret Rey (1906)

17 Gary Paulsen (1939)

20 Mary Pope Osborne (1949)

22 Arnold Lobel (1933)

23 Margaret Wise Brown (1910)

29 Andrew Clements (1949)

June

2 Freddy Adu (1989)

5 Richard Scarry (1919)
6 Cynthia Rylant (1954)
Larisa Oleynik (1981)
Tim Berners-Lee (1955)
9 Freddie Highmore (1992)
10 Maurice Sendak (1928)
Tara Lipinski (1982)
11 Joe Montana (1956)
13 Tim Allen (1953)
15 Jack Horner (1946)
18 Chris Van Allsburg (1949)
25 Eric Carle (1929)
26 Nancy Willard (1936)
Derek Jeter (1974)
Michael Vick (1980)
30 Robert Ballard (1971)
Michael Phelps (1985)

July

2 Dave Thomas (1932)
6 George W. Bush (1946)
7 Lisa Leslie (1972)
Michelle Kwan (1980)
11 E.B. White (1899)
Patricia Polacco (1944)
12 Kristi Yamaguchi (1972)
13 Stephanie Kwolek (1923)
14 Peggy Parish (1927)

14 Laura Numeroff (1953)
18 Nelson Mandela (1918)
24 Barry Bonds (1964)
Mara Wilson (1987)
26 Jan Berenstain (1923)
28 Beatrix Potter (1866)
Natalie Babbitt (1932)
Jim Davis (1945)
31 J.K. Rowling (1965)
Daniel Radcliffe (1989)

August

2 Betsy Byars (1928)
3 Tom Brady (1977)
4 Jeff Gordon (1971)
6 Barbara Cooney (1917)
David Robinson (1965)
9 Patricia McKissack (1944)
Whitney Houston (1963)
11 Joanna Cole (1944)
12 Walter Dean Myers (1937)
Fredrick McKissack (1939)
Ann M. Martin (1955)
15 Linda Ellerbee (1944)
16 Matt Christopher (1917)
18 Paula Danziger (1944)
19 Bill Clinton (1946)

21 Stephen Hillenburg (1961)
23 Kobe Bryant (1978)
24 Cal Ripken Jr. (1960)
26 Mother Teresa (1910)
27 Alexandra Nechita (1985)
28 Brian Pinkney (1961)
29 Temple Grandin (1947)
30 Virginia Lee Burton (1909)
   Sylvia Earle (1935)
   Donald Crews (1938)
31 Itzhak Perlman (1945)

September

1 Gloria Estefan (1958)
3 Aliki (1929)
7 Briana Scurry (1971)
8 Jack Prelutsky (1940)
   Jon Scieszka (1954)
   Jonathan Taylor Thomas (1982)
15 McCloskey, Robert (1914)
   Tomie dePaola (1934)
16 H. A. Rey (1898)
   Roald Dahl (1916)
17 Kevin Clash (1960)
18 Ben Carson (1951)
   Lance Armstrong (1971)

24 Jim Henson (1936)
25 Andrea Davis Pinkney (1963)
25 Will Smith (1968)
26 Serena Williams (1981)
28 Hilary Duff (1987)
29 Stan Berenstain (1923)
30 Dominique Moceanu (1981)

October

1 Mark McGwire (1963)
5 Grant Hill (1972)
   Maya Lin (1959)
6 Lonnie Johnson (1949)
7 Yo-Yo Ma (1955)
8 Faith Ringgold (1930)
9 Zachery Ty Bryan (1981)
10 James Marshall (1942)
11 Michelle Wie (1989)
12 Marion Jones (1975)
13 Nancy Kerrigan (1969)
17 Mae Jemison (1954)
   Nick Cannon (1980)
18 Wynton Marsalis (1961)
   Zac Efron (1987)
22 Ichiro Suzuki (1973)
23 Pele (1940)
25 Pedro Martinez (1971)
26 Hillary Clinton (1947)

Photo and Illustration Credits

Tim Berners-Lee/Photos: Donna Covenev/MIT; Newscom.com.

Miley Cyrus/Photos: copyright © Disney. All Rights Reserved.

Leo and Diane Dillon/Photo: courtesy Harcourt Children's Books. Covers: ASHANTI TO ZULU copyright © 1976 by Leo and Diane Dillon; THE PEOPLE COULD FLY copyright © 2004 by Leo and Diane Dillon; WHY MOSQUITOES BUZZ IN PEOPLE'S EARS copyright © 1975 by Leo and Diane Dillon.

Stephen Hawking/Photos: Simon and Schuster Children's Publishing; Newscom.com. Cover: GEORGE'S SECRET KEY TO THE UNIVERSE copyright © 2007. Courtesy of Simon and Schuster Children's Publishing.

LeBron James/Photos: NBA Photos; Newscom.com.

Richard Peck/Photo: Penguin Putnam Books for Young Readers. Covers: HERE LIES THE LIBRARIAN copyright © 2006 by Richard Peck; A LONG WAY FROM CHICAGO copyright © 1998 by Richard Peck; A YEAR DOWN YONDER copyright © 2000 by Richard Peck.

J.K. Rowling/Photo: Newscom.com. Covers: HARRY POTTER AND THE SORCRER'S STONE copyright © 1997 by J.K. Rowling, Jacket art copyright © 1997 by Mary GrandPre; HARRY POTTER AND THE CHAMBER OF SECRETS copyright © 1999 by J.K. Rowling. Jacket art copyright © 1999 by Mary GrandPre; HARRY POTTER AND THE PRISONER OF AZKABAN copyright © 1999 by J.K. Rowling. Jacket art copyright © 1999 by Mary GrandPre; HARRY POTTER AND GOBLET OF FIRE copyright © 2000 by J.K. Rowling. Jacket art copyright © 2000 by Mary GrandPre; HARRY POTTER AND THE ORDER OF THE PHOENIX copyright © 2003 by J.K. Rowling. Jacket art copyright © 2003 by Mary GrandPre; HARRY POTTER AND THE HALF-BLOOD PRINCE copyright © 2005 by J.K. Rowling. Jacket art copyright © 2005 by Mary GrandPre; HARRY POTTER AND THE DEATHLY HALLOWS copyright © 2007 by J.K. Rowling. Jacket art copyright © 2007 by Mary GrandPre.

REF 920   BIO Fall'07
Biography for beginners :
sketches for early readers.
PV12